EAGLE VISION

EAGLE VISION

MONIFA ROBINSON GROOVER

Vision Publishing House

Vision Publishing House, LLC
P.O. Box 60393
Savannah, GA 31420
Phone: 678-631-9913
Website: www.withinyourreach.org
Twitter: @WYRInspires

Publisher's Cataloging-in-Publication Data
Groover, Monifa Robinson
Eagle Vision. by Monifa Robinson Groover.
72 pages cm.
ISBN: 978-0-9836776-4-2 paperback
        978-0-9836776-5-9 ebook
        978-0-9836776-6-6 ebook
1. Character. 2. Influence. 3. Goal Setting. I. Title
2016935059

TABLE OF CONTENTS

ACKNOWLEDGEMENTS

Jamie Groover

Words cannot adequately express my gratitude toward you. It is an honor and a privilege to be connected with you on this journey. Thank you for your commitment dedication and loyalty. I have learned so much from you and look forward to our future together. You are truly a man beyond measure and a husband beyond compare.

I love you!

Family / Friends / Loved Ones

To my mom (Alice Robinson) and sister (Karima Lane)... Thank you for all your prayers and support.

In loving memory of my dad (Tommy Lee Robinson)... I Love You! You Are Missed!

To All Those Who Have Accompanied Me On This Journey...
It is refreshing to know that in a world so chaotic, God has divinely placed individuals in my life who have deposited seeds of wisdom and encouragement into me. While there are too many to name, I want to thank each of you for you individual gifts of love and support.

Vishal Jetnarayan & the eGenCo Team: Thank you for sharing your insight, wisdom, talent and support. You are awesome. Because of you, the publishing process has been positive, energizing and exciting.

VISION, CHARACTER & STRENGTH

Operating With Excellence

Knowledge, skills and abilities vs. vision, character and strength. Often times the first set of qualities get confused with the latter. There are a number of people who possess knowledge, skills, and abilities but vision, character and strength are attributes that you must show by your actions, and must continuously be upheld. The two sets of qualities, while completely separate, have the ability to work congruently not only to propel you to the top, but keep you there. The top of what, you ask? Well, that is for you to answer. This book is not designed to speak only to those interested in climbing the corporate ladder. It speaks to any and everyone who is curious about what it takes to operate with excellence in any area of their life. Whether it's motherhood, academics, athletics, spiritual growth or personal development, you must raise the standard and operate in excellence if you want to achieve greatness. So it is up to you to decide what "the top" represents in your life. Whatever that is, this book is not only designed to help you activate excellence in your life, but will also teach you to carry it out with integrity.

So what is the difference between the two sets of qualities? Can knowledge, skills and abilities be placed on the same platform as vision, character and strength? The first set of attributes describe someone who is able to perform, whether they studied or were gifted with the ability to do so. These qualities come with fewer expectations than the latter. Vision, character and strength on the other hand are quite different. The risks and expectations placed on the individual who upholds them, can be far greater than most imagine. Integrity and accountability are required to operate with excellence and one cannot fall short of the two. They are the two main things that separate these two sets of traits. There is a tremendous amount of weight and responsibility that come along with having vision, character and strength; at times an undue amount of pressure. That isn't to say people don't have integrity and accountability, only just that it is difficult to find those who not only have it but operate in it to the fullest simply because the humanity of the world we live in leads most to operate in greed and selfishness. It also takes an enormous amount of *courage* to operate with integrity.

Our culture has groomed us in such a way that we think we are operating with excellence and in integrity, however we are not truly aware of how self-centered our ways have become. It takes courage to walk uprightly as well as a certain kind of boldness, particularly when "evil" takes a stance of 'bravado arrogance'. In today's world, those who promote evil whether by their actions or direct intent seem to have the audacity to push its agenda to the fullest. It often leaves me to wonder why the "good" in the world rarely takes its rightful position. It is a case of *good vs evil*.

Once again, it's not about knowledge, skills and abilities being invaluable or ineffective in their own right. Its about raising the standard. We should take these qualities and combine them with vision, character and strength; knowing that the combination of these is explosive (in a good way) and will not only propel you to the top but keep you there.

It is important not to allow your knowledge, skills and abilities to take you where your vision, character and strength can't keep you. This book is about seeing farther, digging deeper and standing taller. So many people have been gifted with the ability to amass and store extreme amounts of information in their brain and take this information and use it to their advantage. They are able to *acquire* skills, whether self-learned

It is important not to allow your knowledge, skills and abilities to take you where your vision, character and strength can't keep you.

or taught by others. They are able to take their *knowledge* and acquired skills and show they have the power and capability to put all this into action, thus proving their *ability*. Most people have the ability to do this at varying degrees. While all this is great, I do have some concerns.

Obtaining knowledge, acquiring skills or showing our capabilities is not a bad way to reflect the traits, however we live in a world where this is necessary if you want to function and achieve some level of success. At the most basic level, some form of knowledge, skills and abilities is required to survive. It is concerning that often times we reach various goals or achieve a certain status in life based on our knowledge skills and abilities and at best, these qualities speak to our ability to 'fit in' within the norm. It speaks to one's ability to manipulate a particular system, to meet the necessary requirements and at times exceed them in order to simply get the job done.

There are many individuals in place and institutions designed to teach us how to meet the status quo, however there are very few individuals and institutions designed to help us exceed them. There are few things in place that

Live beyond the status quo. coach us on how to live up to a standard that is rare. That is what Eagle Vision is about. It is about helping you live beyond the status

quo and moving beyond your comfort zone. As a result, you will reach YOUR top and hold that position with integrity. This is why vision, character and strength are so important. These are the qualities that help you hold your position with integrity. Eagle Vision is about your ability to see what the average person cannot; to exude

Hold your position with integrity. courage, stand firm on what is right even in the face of wrong and the ability to stand, even when you feel your knees

buckling under the pressure.

When we look at one's ability to see farther, dig deeper and stand taller, we are ultimately talking about vision, character and strength. These qualities go beyond the superficial level. Vision, character and strength speak to the depth of one's inner disposition. It speaks to parts that truly make you stand out as an individual. Sometimes these qualities are subtle, to the point where others may not know initially what it is but they recognize something is different about you. Have you ever been somewhere in a crowd of people and someone comes to you and says that you are different from the rest? I used to teach as an adjunct professor and I remember teaching a course on counseling skills. I noticed throughout the course that one student in particular stood out to me. There was nothing about her outward appearance that made her significantly different from the other students but there was something about her character that made her stand apart. Yes, she had knowledge, skills and abilities just like the other students, but there was something about her character that said she was designed to go farther than the rest. There was something inside her that screamed, "I was designed to exceed the status quo!" Not only career-wise but character-wise.

Eagles are a perfect visual of what this book is designed to accomplish. What's so special about the eagle? The eagle is a fascinating bird that possesses unique qualities. In my experience, it is among the elite as far as birds are concerned. I took the time to study various characteristics of the eagle and found that the eagle has some very exclusive characteristics that warrant our attention. While the eagle has many qualities that will be discussed throughout the book, one image that immediately comes to mind is an eagle in flight. Have you ever dreamed of flying like the eagle? Soaring above life's problems and circumstances by spreading your wings and elevating to reach your goals to make your dreams become a reality? Many people say they want to fly high so they can feel the freedom that comes with having no limits or boundaries in the air. So the eagle and humans have something in common; both have it in their nature to live in freedom with a sense of weightlessness. While observing an eagle as it soars, a master of flight, it illustrates these characteristics with ease.

The eagle is a unique and majestic bird. Eagles have a certain precision with the way they operate during their lives; a parallel can be drawn from this to how we can choose to walk out our own lives with high character. It was once so valued and respected it was considered an endangered species. What does this tell us? When you exude certain qualities you will be considered unique. High character individuals will be few and far between in the world, so they often feel alone. Even though the eagle was once an endangered species, it never stopped thriving. It always did what it was designed to do. Now reports say they are no longer considered endangered. This tells me we can beat the odds! I have found that adopting traits that the eagle possesses will be required of us if we are sincere about experiencing breakthroughs in different areas of life and excelling past the status quo. Regardless of your current status this book is designed to catapult you to the next level, if you are ready to do the work!

CHAPTER 1

PERCEPTION & INFLUENCE

Your Future Lies Within

We cannot adequately talk about eagle vision without talking about your future. How do you envision yourself in the future? What causes you to see yourself and your future the way you do? When you ask yourself these questions you are really talking visualizing through your perception. Perception is the way a person judges something based on his personal experience, understanding, and awareness. Perception and vision are inextricably linked, so one cannot be discussed without commentary on the other. What you see and why you see it is critical to the process.

What you see and why you see it is critical to the process.

Influence

Influence is nothing more than the capacity or power of persons or things to be a compelling force on or produce effects on the actions, behavior, or opinions of others. The thing about influence is that it does not need to be overt. It can and is often times subtle. I can think of countless times in the past, when I started singing a song, days after I heard it somewhere and had to stop and ask myself why I was singing it, when it had not been playing at that actual moment?

Everyone is influenced by someone or something. No matter how independent we think we are, we have constant exposure to influences that surround us on a daily basis. The very nature of society sends a continuous flow of stimuli outward which one cannot escape easily, if at all. Some people beg to differ and would argue that they are their own person, they make their own decision and no one thinks for them. Well, the truth of the matter is even they came to that conclusion based on certain experiences they had in the past, whether they realize they have been outwardly affected or not. Whether it was watching how their family member or loved one was manipulated and controlled, or seeing someone with a free spirit live their lives without a care in the world. It may have been something they saw in the media. Either way, the truth is, they did not come to that conclusion on their own. Something they experienced impacted their decision.

Influence is not a bad thing. Just as others have influenced us, all of us in some way want to be influential to others and make an impact on their lives. Think about it - when you have a disagreement with a friend, and both of you go back and forth to state your opinion. Most of the time its not simply because you want the other person to know how you feel, it's usually because you want the other person to have a change of heart regarding the matter. You want them to alter their views on the subject. Influence only becomes a problem when someone is attempting to push a negative agenda or intentionally manipulate a person or situation. When this occurs, it is a recipe for disaster.

One of the reasons you are probably reading this book is because you are a leader at heart and what do leaders do? They attempt to influence others. Whether you are leading your children and training them to become positive and productive members of society, spear-heading a major marketing campaign for a Fortune 500 company or leading a group of people toward having

Influence is connected to your vision.

a deeper spiritual relationship with God, your goal is to influence others. Influence is connected to your vision. It is also connected to your ability to inspire others to change not only by the words you speak but by the life you live.

Sometimes we don't realize how much we have influenced others until much later, just as we don't realize how much others have influenced us, until a significant amount of time has passed. However when you begin to recognize the change in your behavior, or a reaction that came out sideways at another person, or just notice that you acted differently than usual, asking yourself a series of questions will be helpful to identifying any destructive patterns and moving through them. Here are some questions to get you started once you identify that you have reached this point: Who influenced you? What impact they have made in your life and whether it has been positive or negative? You should also determine if your current thoughts and behavior even warrant changing.

Perception

Everyone has a lens through which they view the world and themselves. Did you know that two people can go through the exact same thing and yet each of them can have extremely different experiences? That is because their perceptions are unique to them. Influential people and things in our lives can shape our perception; they can shape the way we judge things. The greater your exposure to the surrounding influences, the greater the risk and/or reward is for influence to occur and potentially take root, whether good, bad or indifferent.

Because everyone sees through a different lens, it is important that we do not set goals based primarily on someone else's perception. This is a slippery slope. There are wise people with excellent perception and it is great to take advice from them. Even when you do accept advice from one who you deem as wise, it is important to do a self-assessment and fine tune your own perception. Everyone has their own experiences, it is possible they may provide feedback that is not the ideal path for you to follow. You must remember their views encompass their life experiences and how they internalized those people and things that influenced them. Here is an example. You may have dreams of being a Neurologist. You may tell your dream to someone who is a Psychologist. Let's say that Psychologist may have constantly struggled in math and science or they may have been great at them, but they may have been told by someone they will never be able to go to school and compete with the other students who are much smarter. They may be inclined to say things that might discourage you from pursuing your dream, even though they may have done this in innocence; not realizing that they are taking their personal interpretation, and projecting it into your dream from an unresolved desire of their own. How they perceive the world, themselves and their situation has a significant impact on how they influence others. So don't allow your dreams to hinge solely on someone else's perception. There will be enough challenges that will combat your own negative thoughts, so you do not need to take on the negative thoughts of others.

Having worked in the counseling and coaching field for many years, I have found that many of my clients embrace worry and self-doubt. What is it about humans, that we find it so difficult to embrace positivity? So often, a person will take one negative thought about themselves and obsess over it. They sit down with a bag of popcorn in a big, comfortable chair and begin to play the scene back in their head as if on a reel, without a pause or a stop button . They will play out the scene until depressed, crying and feeling hopeless. When it comes to something positive they quickly revert back to 'normal', convinced that true joy and happiness cannot exist; thus that particular negative thought wins every time. Heightening one's awareness and paying attention to what is

You do have control over what you embrace. So many people fail to realize how much personal power they have in their own life.

being embraced in thought or in deed is critical. You may not be able to control all the influences that surround you on a daily basis, but you do have control over what you embrace. So many people fail to realize how much personal power they have in their own life. When not recognized and respected, that power is given away when not used properly. Knowing *what* to embrace is essential, and will impact *vision* significantly.

CHAPTER 2

SETTING GOALS

Live Life ON PURPOSE

Eagles are very intentional. They don't operate and live life haphazardly. Strategic by nature, eagles move with deliberation; when they set their sights on something they move with precision and purpose. This is how you must be when attempting to reach your goals. When you set your sights on your goal every move you make towards it must be purposeful. Just like the eagle you must be intentional and each step must be executed with accuracy. Setting goals in life is extremely important. The need for improvement in life is a guarantee for everyone; each individual person has something within themselves that can be improved upon. If we do not move forward and actively work on that which we can improve, we can become stagnant, or stuck, and risk not accomplishing anything (and this can ultimately lead to mental health issues such as depression). Being productive in life helps us live with meaning and purpose, so while we work towards productivity, we can measure it to show our success.

Setting goals is connected to how you see yourself. Your perception and the influences in our lives all play a part in the goal setting process. Many may think setting goals is easy. So why devote an entire chapter to it? Well, if setting goals were so easy, then most people would not have difficulty reaching their goals or making them a reality. Part of the reason most people have difficulty reaching their goals is because the foundational principles of goal setting have not been met. When setting goals, you should be able to answer: Who, What, When, Where, Why and How. Another reason people have difficulty reaching their goals is because they have embraced other people's goals rather than their own. Ask yourself, if you are setting goals based on other people's thoughts or if your goals reflect who you are and the things you want to accomplish.

First let's examine goal-setting a little further. Do your personal goals make you happy? Do you become excited and motivated when you think about your goals? If you set goals to please someone else, chances are you will either be miserable during the process and unsatisfied when you reach your goal or you will fail in your attempt. Your heart has to be in it. If you want to become an attorney but you come from a family of doctors and you only pursue your medical degree because of the family legacy, you will be miserable during the process. You have to want it. The reason you have to want it is because life will throw many challenges your way. So if you do not have the desire, you will have a difficult time. If you are pursuing someone else's dream you will have less motivation and you will not be happy. Life is too short to live it any other way.

You have to set SMART Goals. You may have heard of this before. When you are creating your goals make sure you prioritize them. Once you prioritize them make sure you choose the ones that mean the most to you at that moment. The most important goals that are chosen are those that are now the priority. This process is imperative when setting goals, because if you lack moving through a process, you may end up with too many goals or you might find yourself unsuccessful in achieving them; not because you are not capable, but because you are **Prioritizing is essential.** only one person and can only focus on so many things at one time. (So remember prioritizing is essential.)

In addition to being SMART about your goals, you should write them down. I can't stress this enough! You may be thinking: Why should I write my goals down? I will remember them. Writing goals down on paper is a proven method to obtain success in reaching the goals because it becomes a physical manifestation of accountability that motivates the creator to not stop until they are achieved. Writing your goals down is beneficial for several reasons.

Writing your goals down:
* Helps you organize yourself. It's like a To-Do List. It lists everything you need to do to complete the task.

There is something about writing your goals down that increases your chance of executing them.

- Gives you a reference. You are human. You are liable to forget small details. So writing down your goals will allow you to go back and review them from time to time to make sure you are on track.

- Allows you to prioritize your day. When you look at what you want to accomplish you will be able to set small objectives for the day so you can actually achieve your goals. In order to be successful in achieving your goals you must begin with the end in mind. Writing your goals (the end result) down sets everything in motion. It helps you clarify your vision. It also helps you move forward; taking each step with intention.

In order to increase the likelihood of reaching your goals you should share them. You have to use discretion however and share them with the right people. Everyone does not have your best interest at heart, therefore, not just anyone should be privy to your personal dreams. So find the right people and share your goals. You may be thinking your goals are private and they are for your eyes only, and some of them may be, however there are some goals that should be shared. Sharing is important because it helps you remain accountable. It is so easy to set a goal and get lazy about working toward its achievement when no one else knows. It is easier to make excuses and justify stagnant behavior. When others know what you want to accomplish they will want to be part of your motivation.

And you never know who will be in a position to help you achieve your goals. Remember, you cannot do this alone.

Don't back down on setting those goals! It may seem like a lot of work but it is worth it. Goal setting is part of the process. It is required if success is to be imminent. You've got this!

CHAPTER 3

DISTRACTIONS
The Necessary Evil

When I think about the eagle I think about its focus. It is the master at not allowing distractions to overtake its vision. Distractions are designed to divert your attention away from something. Your vision becomes blurred when too many distractions get in the way. One distraction may not appear to distort your view too much but what happens when you have multiple distractions at the same time? Life is full of distractions. It is imperative that we learn how to deal with these distractions effectively. What is your distraction? What keeps you from pursuing your dreams? What keeps you from being a better person?

So many people try to avoid distractions thinking they are all bad, but this is where so many people get in trouble. The fact that distractions are inevitable make this a total waste of time. If you spend time trying to avoid distractions, you will never reach your goal because you will find yourself spending more time trying to avoid them versus dealing with them. Avoidance does not help you get rid of the distractions; avoidance only prolongs necessary action. It's kind of like someone who is constantly planning. They plan and then they make contingency plans and then they make contingency plans for the contingency plans. Their days and nights are filled with developing plans and never executing them. At some point planning must end and work must begin. The same with distractions; you cannot avoid them forever. At some point you must deal with them.

Avoidance does not help you get rid of the distractions; avoidance only prolongs necessary action.

Now, I am not against planning. I am a planner! However, I know first-hand how constant planning can impede progress. So the key is not to avoid distractions but to learn how to manage them effectively when they come. So how do you handle them you ask? Simple – the key to effectively deal with distractions is to plan for them. You have to know that distractions are part of the plan. Just like failure is part of success. Truly acknowledging and understanding that distractions will be part of the plan places you in a position where you win! While I believe you can and often times will be caught off-guard by the level of intensity distractions bring, you never have to be completely blindsided.

Naturally there will be times where everything appears seamless and there are no hiccups; should this occur then great! Keep moving! However, should you encounter a distraction don't be shocked. Just remember you knew this would be part of the plan. Most people who don't recognize that distractions are part of the plan spend a considerable amount of time trying to move past the fact that something outside of their control actually happened. These individuals spend a great deal of time in shock and amazement that a distraction occurred before they could even deal with the problem. Then they have to spend time actually working on a solution for the problem. This takes so much time and energy. However, the person who has come to the realization and acceptance that distractions are inevitable, does not spend as much time loathing the fact that a distraction took place, they transition more smoothly toward dealing with the matter at hand.

So don't try to avoid distractions and don't become too overwhelmed when distractions come. How do you handle distractions? Prioritize them. Think of it like medical care. Most medical facilities have three foundational levels of care. Within each level you have other levels of care, but for all intents and purposes, we will just look at the basics. Whenever you get sick, you typically triage yourself to determine what level of care you believe you need at that particular time. You evaluate your symptoms and determine if you need to make a visit to your Primary Care Physician, Urgent Care or the Emergency Room.

Normally if you don't feel your symptoms are too severe, and if you have time and patience along with other priorities, you may opt to call your primary care physician and schedule the next available appointment. If you feel your symptoms are somewhat exacerbated and you don't really have the time and patience to wait for an appointment you may go to urgent care. However, if you determine your symptoms warrant immediate attention, you would head straight to the emergency room.

This is also how you should manage your distractions. Triage your "distraction" and determine what level of care is warranted. Does the matter at hand require immediate attention? Is it urgent? Or can it wait? Often times what I find is that distractions usually fall into the 'primary care' and 'urgent care' categories. Rarely do they truly fall within the emergency room category. Most of the time when they fall into the emergency room category it is because WE place them there. Think of how many people go to the emergency room when they really could have gone to urgent care instead. Even the medical professionals prioritize illnesses that come into the emergency room and they determine who gets seen first. I've experienced it time and time again, someone who enters the emergency room with chest pains and difficulty breathing will be seen before someone who appears to have a common cold; even if the person with the common cold arrived first. The point is, not everything is an emergency.

The question you should ask yourself is how do you view distractions? Whether you live in a fairytale world where you think distractions never occur, or you know you are easily distracted, your view of how you see distractions is critical to your outcome. The answer to this question or viewpoint may not always change the result of your situation but it is guaranteed to change you! As previously discussed, perception is a key piece to how you see your world around you, and your perception becomes the 'viewpoint' you adopt. It will make you better or bitter, it will improve your character or diminish it; either way, your personal viewpoint is guaranteed to position you for the next level or keep you stagnant.

Often times we are so focused on the outcome changing that we forget the bigger picture. Even when you can't change the outcome, you can change yourself, and then guess what?... somehow the outcome seems to change.

If you are truly honest with yourself, you might agree that you are your own biggest distraction. Your views and perceptions pose the biggest hindrance to your success. Sure it's easier to cast blame on someone else, but the truth of the matter is, if you want to go to the next level and excel, you have to take full responsibility for your role. Everything that happens to you is not always a result of someone else's actions. Most of the time, it is a result of your own. Once you reach adulthood you must own up to the fact that you are where you are in life because of the decisions you made in the past.

I know this may sound crazy, but sometimes we allow distractions. Sometimes we create distractions because we are afraid of our own success; a fear of moving in excellence due to the challenges of the higher standard we have created. Others look on with a critical eye as if they are just waiting for the 'excellent ones' to fall, because manipulation and greed seem to be the 'norm' of our culture, rather than integrity. Operating with excellence requires you to operate with integrity and sometimes that can be daunting - particularly when society in general operates at a sub-standard level. Do not become the roadblock to personal progress. Learn to manage distractions effectively. DON'T let them manage you!

CHAPTER 4

VISION

I Can See Clearly Now

"Eyes that look are common, eyes that see are rare"
- J. Oswald Sanders

Ah! Here we are, faced with the question of whether we should run with the crowd or walk the road less traveled? I will admit running with the crowd and doing what everyone is doing appears to have its advantages - there is safety in numbers. Going along with the crowd allows you to stay under the radar, never being identified as unique or 'different' and allows you rely heavily on the gifts and talents of others, never having to take the risk of others seeing you fail. These appear to be great benefits right? Well, I am not sure whether these are advantages or disadvantages. It makes me question if blending in with the crowd brings opportunities or if it is a subtle, **If you are going to rise to the eagle's standard you must remember that you are rare.**

unconscious way designed to stunt your growth.   You will never fit in with the crowd no matter how hard you try. You will always be noticed for the unique qualities you possess.

There is a level of safety and predictability associated with being and doing what is common. My question to you is: Is common what you really want to be? I am going to take a risk and say, that because you have gotten this far in reading this book, then the answer is most likely 'no'. You recognize you were not born to be common, nor were you born to 'run with the pack'. You were born to stand out, to lead and truly "see". J. Oswald Sanders said it so eloquently, "Eyes that look are common, eyes that see are rare." Eagle vision is rare. You were born to be rare.

There are so many people who can look but very few can actually see. To "look" means to direct your eyes in a particular direction. To "see" is to become aware of, or have insight and foresight into something. Many people have the ability to fixate their eyes on something but so few have the ability to see beyond the surface.

Here is a scenario to help illustrate between 'sight' and 'vision'. When a mother and child walk into a candy store, the child is fixated on all the candy he just encountered. Nothing else in the world matters in that moment. He grabs at everything his little hands can hold while constantly reaching for more. All he takes note of is how wonderful his life will be now that he has entered Candyland! Oh, but the mother is completely different. Having some age and wisdom, she looks past the actual candy and "sees" everything attached to it. The mother would probably do almost anything to make her child happy.

However, she is tasked with the responsibility of guiding her child in the right direction and sometimes there is a conflict between the two. She knows that allowing her child to eat as much candy as he wants would make the child happy yet, she is also aware that too much candy will ultimately cause a stomach ache, nausea, cavities, challenges with obesity, diabetes and high cholesterol just to name a few. She sees the bigger picture around the present moment. So with this vision and ability to "see" she must proceed with caution.

That is how adults can be at times. Adults can become so fixated on something; something that will give immediate pleasure that is either not recognized or that is ignored when the consequences are attached. Vision is looking into the future to see what the end result will be and make our decisions from that frame of reference. There is a quote by Stephen Covey that says, "Begin with the end in mind." If we do this, we strategically place ourselves in a position where we will accomplish our goals and experience success. True vision is about keeping the end in mind from the beginning throughout the entire process. Your ability to clearly see your destination enhances your chances in getting there. Without clear vision you are liable to end up anywhere. Your ability to see beyond your current circumstance is critical to whether or not you will die, survive or thrive.

We are a microwave society, literally and figuratively. This is one of our downfalls as a society. We are constantly *told* by society to set goals but we are trained to do everything in our power to short-circuit the process. Our culture tells us to 'dream big'. Children are told they can do anything they want to do; the sky is the limit. They are told that it takes time and hard work to achieve their dream, but the message is really contradicting, in that people are urged to take short-cuts as often as possible to get ahead quicker. Ultimately, we are taught to try and find a way to produce the same results without actually putting in any work. Of course there are people who actually put in the work it takes for success, but they are easily the minority. For the most part, we are taught that everything is supposed to come *right now*. It doesn't quite work that way. If you try to short circuit the system you will end up like the hamster on the wheel, constantly running but never really getting anywhere.

We have become so impatient that we can't even wait for our food to heat up on top of the stove. We heat it up in the microwave despite all the reports about health consequences. If we are honest with ourselves, depending on our hunger level, the microwave is even too slow. I have taken food out of the microwave before it got hot and started eating it because I simply could not wait an extra thirty seconds. How crazy is that? We want what we want and we want it now, despite the consequences but we still have an expectation of having high quality. The truth is food reheated on top of the stove tastes much different than food reheated in the microwave. That burger I make at home tastes totally different than the one I purchase from the drive-thru at the fast food restaurant. They are both burgers but the quality is not the same.

Another thing about vision is that it is yours. Too often we give our power away. I am convinced many

No one can take away your vision. of us use the word can't, not because we have always inherently believed we can't, but because others have somehow convinced us our goals are impossible to reach. Think about how fearless children are; they rarely see obstacles, they see opportunities. They usually only hesitate when adults tell them not to do something. From a young age children are told they 'can't'. *You can't climb that tree because you might fall; you can't do back flips because you might break your neck.* Then we wonder why as adults they have so many reservations about life and reaching for their dreams. That is because the influences in their lives taught them they can't accomplish anything that appears challenging or appears to have any consequences attached. They have been told all their lives they should not make any attempts to reach the goals that appear to fall outside other people's comfort zone. Now, as adults they have to battle with what I call the 'I can't syndrome'.

Eagle Vision

Let's take a closer look at the eagle and its vision. Let's determine what type of vision it takes to reach our goals and operate in excellence and integrity. The eagle's vision is sharp, clear - superior. It far surpasses man's vision. Taking a closer look will help define why it is wise to sharpen your vision.

Researchers who study the eagle will tell you that if you ever have the opportunity to watch an eagle closely while it sits on a mountain or in a tree you will notice how attentive this bird is to its family and home[1]. Its body normally sits still and its head will tilt from side to side taking careful observation to what is happening below, around and above it. Eagles have very keen vision. Their eyes are specifically designed for long distance focus. They can spot another eagle soaring from 50 miles away.

Vision is about your ability to "see" not "look". This represents depth of perception at its finest. This means their insight and their ability to see extends far beyond the average bird. Just like the eagle, our ability to see ahead is crucial to the process.

Did you know the eagle has a clear membrane that glides across its eyeballs? This membrane is designed to clear debris similar to the human eyelid. This is amazing because while human eyelids are designed for a similar purpose, unlike the eagle, for less than a millisecond, we cannot see when we blink. This is such a short period of time and many would say this does not affect our vision and our ability to see, but I believe every moment counts, so I often wonder if that millisecond really does affect our vision?

The eagle's vision is very sharp and clear. When your vision is clear there is a certain level of confidence that exudes from knowing what is in front of you, or what is coming. Having clear vision is necessary for the

---

[1]   If you would like to watch a real eagle in action, please visit www.georgiawildlife.com/BerryEagleCam for live footage.

process but the clarity you seek must begin within. Let me explain. Have you ever had a question or been confused about something and decided to ask everyone in your address book what they thought about the matter? Confusion sets in with varying opinions and thoughts that make it more difficult to understand. The reason for this confusion is because when you have no clarity yourself prior to seeking out answers from others, you are already double-minded (meaning that you waver more easily in your understanding and keep going back and forth instead of making a decision). Once you invite five other people with their own perspectives into the matter, some of whom have no clarity themselves, you have ordered an additional plate of chaos with a side of confusion. Without clear vision you will remain stagnant and risk being stuck in the same place, and you almost assuredly will remain in a confused and unsure state of mind.

I have learned when I am in a dilemma, it is better for me to ponder over the situation myself first before presenting it to others. Even if I don't come up with a solid answer right away, the point is I searched within myself first. When I do present the matter to others I use discretion regarding to whom I should speak, and even then I am careful about the feedback and advice I internalize.

When it comes to handling situations or seeking guidance from others, it is important to examine your values and come to some conclusions on where your values lie before seeking out counsel. You may not have all the answers but it is important to establish your thoughts, beliefs and values regarding the matter at hand. If you don't you will be easily swayed by everyone else's beliefs.

There is a delicate balance between having a sense of clarity within and being open minded enough to accept information and feedback from others. There is a certain level of maturity and discernment that comes along with this. You have to be able to determine when to take the risk of walking in someone else's wisdom even when you are not sure what to do next or how to respond to the situation. This is one reason why it is important to surround yourself with the right people.

Having blurred vision is not fun and it is very uncomfortable. I wear glasses. When I take my glasses off my vision becomes very blurry. It is a very uncomfortable feeling to say the least. I can see objects up close but please don't ask me to identify anything more than 5 feet away. I would immediately squint and make faces that would be fitting for America's Funniest Videos! Seeing with clarity not only helps you get to your personal 'top' but it is critical in helping you stay there and occupy that space with integrity and accountability

Having clear vision means you have the ability to easily perceive, understand, or interpret something. When your vision is clear things become transparent, and it takes a lot to get you off-course. It can be a cloudy day and the way seems bleak, but as long as you have clear vision you are okay. You realize the storm may alter your course but it does not alter your destination. It alters the plan so the vision will manifest. Having clear vision has more to do with your

The storm may alter your course but it does not alter your destination.

internal thought process than your external circumstances. As a graduate of Clark Atlanta University our motto was "I'll find a way or make one".

In addition to sharp, clear sight, the eagle also has *broad* vision. This is important because it allows the eagle to see its enemy coming even when it is focused on something specific. If the eagle operated with tunnel vision this would cripple its ability to guard itself against the enemy. We are physically designed the same way. It's called peripheral vision. Peripheral vision is defined as having the ability to see everything that is visible to the eye, outside the central area of focus. It is also referred to as side vision. Having the ability to focus while being able to determine possible danger is important. Imagine driving without peripheral vision. Imagine walking down the street with blinders on, only having the ability to see directly ahead. If you did not have this ability you would have to turn your head full-circle before being able to make your next move safely. This would be uncomfortable and even cumbersome.

Eagles see colors more vividly than humans, and can differentiate between more color shades and actually see ultraviolet. This particular variance gives eagles keen eyesight that enables them to spot even well-camouflaged, potential prey from a very long distance. Their vision is expansive – almost panoramic. Imagine having the ability to do this as a human. This is how your vision must be if you are going to be able to successfully navigate the challenges ahead. When you have the ability to soar to heights far above the average person your vision must be broad. People may become jealous and try to bring you down. They may try to attack your self-esteem, your character and your abilities. You have to maintain broad vision and determination if you are destined to succeed.

Eagles have a unique ability to remain focused and lock their sights on anything in the moment. If you watch an eagle, you will not see too much movement. Every move the eagle makes is strategic. If you are going to remain focused, you must remain still. What does this mean? This means you cannot be easily swayed by every wind. You have to have clear vision, patience and the ability to be still. Focus requires only necessary, strategic movement.

Sometimes remaining focused is a challenge. Distractions may arise, and you may feel it is taking a long time to achieve your end result. Despite your passion, you may have times when you experience a loss of motivation. There are so many things that may keep you from remaining focused and moving forward. One of the things I make sure I do often is surround myself with others who have qualities I admire; those who work diligently to achieve their goals. It is important to surround yourself with people who have drive, are committed and those who are determined to make things happen. One thing I know for sure is that no matter how motivated I am on my own, my level of motivation soars exponentially when I surround myself with others who work diligently to meet their goals. When I surround myself with others who have qualities I admire I am somehow automatically energized to think bigger and soar higher. Often times you hear people talk about putting together a team for businesses or a team for athletics or an academic study group team. The reason is because there is power in a team. One person cannot do everything alone. This same concept holds true for us personally when it comes to focus and motivation. While a large part of focus is our own personal responsibility, having like-minded people around is very helpful.

CHAPTER 5

CHARACTER

Integrity...
The Ultimate Sign of Maturity

"You express the truth of your character with the choice of your actions." -Steve Marabol

Everyone is ultimately propelled towards truth, and our spirit recognizes it immediately. We may not always like what the truth presents to us in the moment but that doesn't change the fact that the truth cannot be altered. You can try and cover it up or manipulate it, but truth will inevitably shine. One way that truth identifies itself purely, is through actions. It is a matter of motive. People will not do something unless it is in their heart to do it and there is always a purpose or motive to explain the behavior. It is a well-known saying that 'actions speak louder than words.' For example, someone who constantly tells others that they should behave in a certain way, but then behaves directly opposite of what he preached would be known as a hypocrite. His actions directly contradict what his mouth says. Eventually, he will become known by this title by those who see the contradiction play out time and time again. The only way to change this image, is change his behavior so it matches what he says to others or what he preaches. Then and only then will the truth of his character change. This takes time to repeatedly show oneself approved and eventually, he will become known as 'a man of his word'.

We have control over the image we project to others. We cannot control how others receive and conceptualize that image, but we have the ability to choose what we want others to see. Too often we give our power away. When a situation occurs, you determine how you will respond. You are responsible for yourself. So many people cast blame towards others to find an excuse for the reason they did or said something. If you don't remember anything else you must remember this: ultimately you and only you are responsible for your decisions. You may be influenced by others, but you are still held accountable for your final actions. What truth do you want others to see? What truth do you want them to experience?

Ultimately you and only you are responsible for your decisions.

Let's talk a little more about character. Character is the moral qualities distinctive to an individual. Simply put, character is the way someone thinks, feels, and behaves; someone's personality. So what did Marabol mean when he said "You express the truth of your character with the choice of your actions." One interpretation is that you can identify character within a person by their behavior. Determining one's character through behavior (actions) is merely one step beyond the contradiction between their words and behavior. Here is an example. If someone walks out of a grocery store, and unloads the groceries into their car, then leaves the shopping cart at the front of their car instead of actually putting it into the cart return, that shows someone's character. They may not actually preach to people regularly that they should always put their cart back, but the fact that they did not respect property that was not theirs enough to put it where it would not get further damaged, shows they lack something in character. It does not mean that they have no character at all, but that one quality of their character could use some work. It goes beyond just not having our words and actions line up, but character is also about practicing excellence even when our words and actions do line up.

Your character and your reputation are what you are known for. Having a good name and exceptional character will not only help you get to the top, but it will help you stay there. It will bring you before people in high places and will draw people to you. This may be a difficult concept to accept because you feel that you pride yourself on having exceptional character, yet you still feel stuck. Your name is good and you are well respected but you can't seem to get anywhere. In your eyes it seems like everyone committed to lying, stealing and cheating gets promoted and somehow

Success cannot be defined by the things we have or societal definitions.

works their way up the ranks, while your good name has you sitting in a corner collecting dust. This is why I am adamant about the fact that success cannot be defined by the things we have or societal definitions. If we use tangible things to define success, we are in trouble. If we defined our success based on the principles of our culture, then most of us would be miserable. Things come and go. Things are temporary. However, the character that is within is what will truly stand the test of time.

Even if you did define success by tangible things, you shouldn't need everybody to recognize your capabilities. You should want the *right* people to recognize them. The right people are those who will honor your good name, your reputation and your vision and help catapult you to the next level so the masses can benefit. Sometimes we become obsessed with wanting everyone to see our greatness. While there is nothing wrong with that, it places you in a very vulnerable position; a position where you seek too much validation from others and where you are likely to compromise your morals and values. Remember, Eagle Vision is not about meeting the status quo, it's about exceeding it. It is about upholding a standard of integrity and being accountable for your actions in truth and beyond to excellence.

When you try to gain everyone's approval you set yourself up for compromise. I believe most people are afraid to operate in integrity. Once you are known for having a character of honesty and integrity, people place expectations on you. You are now accountable for your actions. This wouldn't be so bad if you did not live in a society that appears to honor dishonesty and promote those who lack integrity. Being identified as a person with integrity forces you to maintain a standard that others normally shy away from. If you are determined to have the character of an eagle you must realize that you will be alone more often than you would like. This is the road less traveled. Let's delve some more into the eagle's character.

Eagle Character

Eagles are not scavengers, so they do not feed on dead things. Why is this important to note? It is important because a lot of times humans have difficulty embracing change. Sometimes we have a difficult time letting go of the past and releasing dead things. Opportunity could be staring us in the face yet we will second guess whether or not we should proceed forward because we know doing so will require change and possibly leaving some people, places or things behind. It will require us to leave our old way of thinking and our old behavior in the past. When it comes down to it, the problem is that people have difficulty with change because it requires that they go beyond their comfort zone.

In order to elevate and move beyond your situation, you have to elevate your mind. For some it is better to deal with the consequences of the same old mess instead of dealing with the fear of the unknown. If you are going to soar like an eagle, you have to be willing to soar into unknown, unchartered territory. Eagles fly higher into places other birds would not dare

You will not be able to feed the vision with your old mindset.

go, but they must leave some things behind and seek out new adventures. You will have to do the same if you ever want to soar to higher heights. You will not be able to feed the vision with your old mindset. What you put into it is exactly what you will get out of it.

Solitude

We are designed to connect and interact with others. Most people function best when they have family, friends and loved ones around. Despite this fact, there are times where we should all have moments of solitude. This is important to note because the eagle in all its wisdom, respects the importance of taking time to itself to regenerate and re-energize.

When the eagle gets to be around thirty years old, it is considered old and its body will not function and fly the way it use to. Their feathers become worn out, which slows down their ability to soar at high speeds and maneuver effectively in the air. So it makes a decision to go into hiding in the mountains where it begins to pluck its feathers off its body and wings until their entire body is laid bare. After about five months when their body regenerates and the feathers come back, the eagle comes out of seclusion with the ability to fly dynamically and royally again without much effort. This then allows the eagle to live another 30-40 years. This gives us insight into what solitude is really about. It tells us solitude necessary in order to keep the vision alive. Just as the eagle can only do this in solitude, there are many things that can only be accomplished in solitude for us. Sometimes we can only get what we need by making a conscious effort to be alone and reflect. For someone it may be a stay-cat-ion. For another person it may be a trip to the beach. For another it may be a trip to the mountains. Whatever it is for you, do it - and without apology. You need to take care of yourself. Remember the vision is only as good as the visionary.

Flies Only With Eagles

I guess the old saying is correct "Birds of a feather flock together." Eagles are known to flock with other eagles. They enjoy flying together at high altitudes. Eagles don't normally mix with other birds. You probably won't find too many eagles mingling with chickens.

Not that there is anything bad about chickens, but the eagle and the chicken have a different build and as a result, the chicken will never soar as high or as freely as the eagle.

You do, however, have to be careful about the company you keep. There are many people who have been known to have good character but because they continued to surround themselves with others who displayed a lack thereof, they found themselves making decision they would not have otherwise made. In doing so, many people have gotten arrested, been significantly injured or endured negative consequences as a result of their deci-sions. 'Bad company corrupts good charac-ter,' (1 Corinthians 15:33 NIV). No matter how gifted you are, if you remain around others who refuse to use their gifts for

'Bad company corrupts good character,' (1 Corinthians 15:33 NIV).

good, you will eventually find yourself doing the same. But if you surround yourself with people who are determined to soar you will find yourself soaring beyond your wildest dreams.

When you are committed to accomplishing great things it is necessary to surround yourself with greatness. You cannot learn what it takes to become an awesome parent hanging around others who don't care about their own children. You must connect with like-minded people. Your circle should consist of those on your level, those trying to get where you are and those who have been where you are trying to go. Within that circle you will find everyone can help the next person and receive help in so many ways. Interdependency with like-minded people is necessary for success.

Interdependency with like-minded people is necessary for success.

CHAPTER 6

STRENGTH

Strong and Steady Wins The Race

"Courage doesn't always roar. Sometimes courage is a
quiet voice at the end of the day saying
'I will try again tomorrow'" - Mary Ann Radmacher

Eagle vision is not about outward strength. It is about
inner strength and qualities that stand the test of time.
Inner strength is not something others give you, nor is it
something that can be wrapped up in a pretty package
and placed under a Christmas tree. Inner strength is
discovered, fine-tuned and matured as you travel along
this journey of life. The principles can be taught but only
time and experience provide you with the opportunity
to grow. Strength is about courage and endurance, not
about what circumstances look like, especially when there
is clear vision. I will find a way and if I don't succeed
today, if given the opportunity, I will try again tomorrow.

Mary Ann Radmacher said it so eloquently when she said, "Courage doesn't always roar. Sometimes courage is a quiet voice at the end of the day saying 'I will try again tomorrow'." Courage is the ability to make difficult or challenging decisions in the face of danger, fear or pain. It's not always about doing something daring like jumping out of an airplane. Sometimes it takes courage to do the right thing. Especially when you are around a large group of people who are doing the wrong thing. It takes courage to operate in integrity when others don't. Being courageous is really about inward conviction and commitment. Courageous people often have nights of solitude when they question their next move and evaluate themselves and their motives. Courage is

Courage is about facing yourself more than it is about facing others.

about facing yourself more than it is about facing others. It's about staring your own inadequacies in the face and making the decision to deal with those inadequacies while continuing to move forward. It is about being able to maintain high self-esteem even when your weakness appears to take a front row seat. When we think of courageous people often times we have grand thoughts of someone standing in the lion's cage trying to tame a lion. I have found that sometimes the most courageous people are the ones who don't take center stage; they are the ones who sit in the quiet and make the decision to live and not take their life despite their strong desire to die.

When you look at body builders you see their physical power and strength. Their muscles are fit and toned; they have about zero percent body fat and their muscles seem to bulge out of their bodies. It is obvious they worked long and hard to reach this fitness level. In order to maintain this level of fitness I am quite sure they have to maintain the proper exercise and nutrition plan. They have to be committed to health and wellness despite the many temptations available to them. If it takes commitment to keep the outward appearance looking great, imagine what it takes to maintain your commitment to foster a better you from the inside out. Inner strength works the same way.

By nature, eagles undergo a process that is necessary for them to remain strong, or regain their strength in life. They understand your strength can **You have to** fade easily and quickly if you are not **be committed.** careful. But you have to be committed to the process. You have to be committed to standing in front of the mirror daily and staring the challenges in the face with determination to win. Let's look more closely at the eagle's strength both inward and outward.

Eagle Strength

The eagle does not exhibit fear. The eagle is determined and will never surrender to its prey or give up a fight. It is not intimidated by the size of its enemy. Those things are irrelevant to the eagle. What does this tell us? It tells us that we must be prepared to encounter storms that appear overwhelming. We must be prepared to fight and not give up, even when the process is not easy. But when the pressure comes, it is important to stand your ground and not buckle under the pressure.

Being fearless is really about perseverance. Perseverance is required if you stand any chance of reaching your goals. To the eagle there is no other way than how it was created to be so it does what it needs to survive. In the example of the eagle's perseverance, if there is no resolve or determination to come out on top, you are less likely to achieve your goals. Being fearless speaks to the amount of courage you have that allows you to look adversity square in the eyes and not back down.

The eagle is also courageous. Remember, courage is really about the ability to look within and face the truth about yourself. While the eagle does have weaknesses, it does not allow its weaknesses to overshadow its strengths. Here are some of the eagle's weaknesses:

- Because of it's royal and majestic look, eagles are easily identified by hunters, so they lack the ability to blend in well, causing them to be in constant danger.
- Some bald eagles seek out and eat salmon in running waters and they gorge themselves on spawning and dying fish to the point they can no longer fly or move quickly. This makes them vulnerable to other predators like bears.

Also, because they are relatively heavy birds, sometimes they can drown to death or die of hypothermia if they plunge too far into the water while fishing.

These are major hurdles the eagle must overcome. The eagle is no stranger to challenges and encounters many problematic scenarios throughout its life; some are a result of human interference, while others are the result of the eagle's natural physique which plays against them in situations where they lack sound judgment. Despite all opposition, the eagle thrives and is still respected as a truly majestic bird.

Despite our challenges, we must take our cues from the eagle and rise above our situation. This is where courage and integrity come into play. It takes heart, it takes bravery and it takes nerve to be courageous when danger and difficulty are staring you in the face.

Built For The Storm

Eagles are built different from many other birds; primarily because of their larger size, more powerful build, heavier head and beak. Their stature suggests royalty. Eagles are physically built to handle storms. Most would think the eagle's build is a disadvantage during storms. Due to its size and weight, a storm would most certainly

The eagle uses it's heavy weight to its advantage in a storm, by locking its wings and using the storm's pressure and power to elevate the eagle higher.

bring the eagle down. This is not the case. It does not allow its weight to become a hindrance to completing its mission. The eagle uses it's heavy weight to its advantage in a storm, by locking its wings and using the storm's pressure and power to elevate the eagle higher.

Be honest with yourself. Would you say that you don't look forward to encountering storms in your life? Who does? Who looks forward to hearing the doctor give a bad report? No one wants bad things to happen. The key however is to be like the eagle, using those circumstances to your advantage. I can't tell you how many testimonies I have heard where people have said losing their job was the best thing that ever happened to them because they finally started their own business, or that the bad report they received from the doctor brought their family closer. They used these situations to catapult them to the next level. But the only way you are going to be successful is if you truly understand you were built for the storm. You must realize the storm is an opportunity and not an opposition.

How do you view the storms in your life? When you encounter a storm, do you die, survive or thrive? Do you think enough of yourself to know that you can make it through the storms of life? You may have a group of people cheering you on but you also have to believe in yourself.

The storm is an opportunity and not an opposition.

Possesses Vitality

We can't forget to mention the eagle's vitality. Vitality is the energy and power to endure. Endurance, perseverance and patience are key. When most people think of energy they think of bouncing off the walls and constant movement. While the eagle does have plenty of power and energy, it goes about generating it in a very unique way. As the eagle undergoes it's transformation around age 30, it gains something in return during this time in solitude – renewed life. This is the purpose for the change, so that the regeneration occurs with vitality and strength as a final result. Once the eagle has completed this process, it almost begins life anew, with proper rest and restoration. Capable of now doubling their life span, this is a great example of true strength. It shows us that strength does not rest solely in physical ability, but in our ability to recognize when we should slow down and regenerate. Endurance is not simply about the ability to do something difficult for a long time, it is about also employing the right strategy so that you see your end result manifest without being totally worn out when you finally do win. Endurance is about knowing how to stay in the race.

Endurance is about knowing how to stay in the race.

It's about knowing how to fight and withstand the storm and being strategic and constantly assessing and re-assessing your strength.

The process the eagle goes through to regain its vitality takes perseverance, patience and time. There is an incubation period that occurs before and sometimes during the process. An incubation period is nothing more than the process of developing slowly without outward or perceptible signs. Things may not always move as fast as we want them to but remember, there is always movement.

One thing I noticed is when the eagle goes into the mountains to regenerate, it goes alone. This is one reason some people shy away from their greatness. They are afraid of the isolation it brings. Even though they know they will have support along the way, they understand this is truly the road less traveled so they rarely want to walk this path. If you want to get to the next level and excel, you must come to understand that there are some things that will have to be done by you alone, in order to accomplish greater strength to rise above the storm. Energy, endurance, perseverance and patience is fostered during this time.

CHAPTER 7

IS IT WORTH IT?

The Fruit of Your Labor

Eagle Vision is about achieving success from the inside out. It is not about your bottom-line but about realizing your true value by seeing your potential and striving for greatness. Eagle Vision gets you to see the big picture and teaches you how to walk out your vision with integrity. First, by acknowledging your knowledge, skills and abilities you will propel to the next level in your life. Building onto that precept, layer on your vision, character and strength while operating in your gifts, and you will achieve excellence.

Those with eagle vision have to deal with what is known as the *iceberg illusion*. When you operate with a certain level of integrity and success all people tend to see are the end results- the tip of the iceberg. Most never know what it really took for someone to get to that uppermost point. Most people only see your strength. They see your character and they see your vision. But just like an iceberg, no one really knows what lies beneath. The only people that know what truly lies beneath are those who seek to soar like an eagle. Some of the challenges faced are failure, disappointment, hard work, dedication, persistence, sacrifice and discipline. The reason eagle vision is rare is because most people don't want to do the work. Most people are not willing to endure the trials that come with success.

In many ways I think the work you have to do in order to obtain inward success is harder. It requires a deeper level of commitment as well as the ability to face your own fears and vulnerabilities. I also believe the rewards are much greater. The benefits that come from fine-tuning your vision, character and strength are beyond compare. The benefits are contagious. People are touched and lives are transformed. So many people have encountered challenges that have taken them to their highest level of vulnerability. The pressures of life have a way of weighing you down and keeping you from reaching your fullest potential. It is easy to fall into the cycle of despair. So when you make the tough decision to pursue greatness you have made a decision to alter your path as well as the path of others for the better. The decision may not be easy but they rewards are great.

Review the characteristics of the eagle. See how you measure up. Remember it is not what lies on the outside that qualifies you as a person of vision, character and strength. It is what lies within. So ask yourself these questions.

Is It Worth It?

How sharp is my vision?
How solid is my character?
How much strength lies within?

Remember, never allow your knowledge, skills and abilities to take you where your vision, character and strength can't keep you!

Additional material and Supplemental Study Guides are available for download at:

Withinyourreach.org

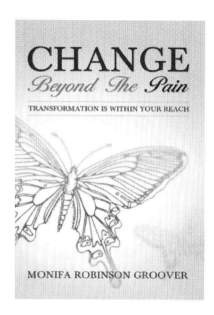

CHANGE
Beyond The Pain

TRANSFORMATION IS WITHIN YOUR REACH

MONIFA ROBINSON GROOVER

The purpose of this manual is to teach you how to transform your life. While this manual is no substitute for the Word of God (The Bible), let this be a guide that simply helps you gain a deeper understanding of what God is trying to impart in all of us.

Change Beyond The Pain will help you discover:

- True healing comes from allowing God to transform your life
- You do not have to revert back to the same cycle of hurt, anger,fear and depression
- God has a plan for your life
- There is power and purpose in your pain

This book will teach you how to move beyond accepting change to embracing transformation. So, if you are seeking restoration, grab your Bible, this book, and open your heart and watch the transformation begin.

This workbook will teach you how to transform your life. Utilizing the strength of the Word of God and this guide as a tool, Change Beyond The Pain will empower you to gain a deeper understanding of what God is trying to impart in all of us.

The Change Beyond The Pain Workbook will help you discover:

- How true healing comes from allowing God to transform your life.
- How to stop repeating the same cycles of hurt, anger, fear and depression.
- That God has a plan for your life.
- There is power and purpose in your pain to help you experience positive and productive transformation.

You will learn how to move beyond accepting change to embracing transformation. So, if you are seeking restoration, read this book with an open heart, and together with your bible let the transformation begin.

Available for purchase at www.withinyourreach.org

Monifa is a well known, highly sought after Author, Speaker and Life Coach. As CEO of Within Your Reach, she is dedicated to helping YOU move beyond your current circumstance and live a healthier, more productive and fulfilling life.

If your are interested in: Life Coaching
Workshops / Seminars
Keynote Addresses
Retreats

Contact Within Your Reach today!

Within Your Reach Consulting Services, LLC
P.O. Box 60393
Savannah, GA 31420
404-271-2685 Office
www.withinyourreach.org

Remember...Always Live Your Life ~ On PURPOSE!

Vision Publishing House, LLC
P.O. Box 60393
Savannah, GA 31420
678-631-9913

Website: www.withinyourreach.org
Twitter: @WYRInspires

Made in the USA
Middletown, DE
02 July 2024

56590499R00040